For Tim, who edited my doubts

For Katie, who edited the words

Introduction

Welcome to this five-week study on the book of Philippians! This powerful little epistle in the New Testament has been nicknamed "the book of Joy" and will hopefully give us the reframe and refreshing we need to move forward with God's perspective in our lives rather than our own. I have prayed that these lessons will provide you with Scripture, knowledge, and insight that you can carry throughout your day as you purposefully and intentionally pursue joy.

For each week, there will be four days of personal study. On each of these days, I encourage you to read through the accompanying verses a couple times on your own before beginning the content of the day's lesson. Ask God for His wisdom and insight and jot down any thoughts that come. God's Word is a living entity, and while I am excited to share what I believe He has given me, I am also curious what He is going to tell you! This devotional will guide you along with my own thoughts and questions, however, the ultimate hope is that you also grow in your own discernment and interpretations. I am excited to journey alongside you through these next five weeks. I have prayed for you as you enter this study.

En-"Joy!"

Week One

Day 1, Background Influence (Self-Awareness)

As I sit here at the computer seeking the words to share with you, it always amazes me that Paul wrote close to a third of the New Testament. While the sheer volume of his work is impressive, the circumstances under which he produced it are even more amazing.

As Paul wrote Philippians, he was sitting in prison after being arrested for the work of the Gospel. While there is some debate about whether this was a true imprisonment or a house arrest, he makes it clear that this was not a comfortable nor enjoyable experience. In the coming weeks, we will learn much about the difficulties Paul faced in his previous journeys as well as the ones he was enduring when he wrote this letter. The dire nature of his circumstances makes it all the more amazing that it is in this letter that he wrote the most about how he cultivated joy. Rather than focusing on all that was not going well in his life, he instead offers direct advice as well as perspectives that allowed him to continue to center himself in Christ during these challenging circumstances.

Before his conversion on the road to Damascus (Acts 9), Paul prided himself on being a Jewish Pharisee and a direct descendant of the twelve tribes of Israel. He became a violent enemy of the Gospel, persecuting members of the early church and speaking out against the God who would eventually become the source of his saving message to the Gentiles. While he had the distinct advantage of being divinely inspired to write Scripture, Paul's experiences influenced the way he shared information with us in the book of Philippians. And so it is with our experiences as we seek to glean information and insight from the Bible. The way we were raised, our experiences with religion, our experiences with others, with love, with loss, how we were taught about why bad things happen and why good people sometimes do bad things…it all affects how we understand information about God and from God.

A strong understanding of the past gives us great wisdom for the future.

Self-awareness is an essential pursuit for any of us who wants to better discern God's thoughts from our own. It is important for us to spend time thinking about what filters have been added to our perspectives to better zero in on the truths God shares with us in the Scriptures. Additionally, an increase in self-awareness can also bring clearer recognition of God's fingerprints on you as a person and His hand in your life. The personality He gave you, the blessings He has given and the difficulties He has allowed, the family He placed you in, the places you have lived, and the experiences you have had all help to point us toward His purpose in our lives and force us to decide what we think about who He is.

I know we haven't gotten to a single portion of Scripture yet, but before we begin, please take a moment and reflect in this area. It is only as we become more self-aware and use the Holy Spirit to discern the world around us that we can begin to see God more clearly.

Reflection Questions:

What life experiences have most influenced how you view God?

_____

_____

_____

_____

_____

In what ways has your understanding of who God is changed over time?

_____

_____

_____

_____

_____

Share a time when you felt God was communicating with you very clearly and how you knew it was His voice rather than your own.

_____

_____

_____

_____

_____

Day 2, *Philippians 1:1-8 (Friendship)*

Paul and Timothy, servants of Christ Jesus, to all God's holy people in Christ Jesus at Philippi, together with the overseers and deacons: ² Grace and peace to you from God our Father and the Lord Jesus Christ.³ I thank my God every time I remember you. ⁴ In all my prayers for all of you, I always pray with joy ⁵ because of your partnership in the gospel from the first day until now, ⁶ being confident of this, that he who began a good work in you will carry it on to completion until the day of Christ Jesus. ⁷ It is right for me to feel this way about all of you, since I have you in my heart and, whether I am in chains or defending and confirming the gospel, all of you share in God's grace with me. ⁸ God can testify how I long for all of you with the affection of Christ Jesus.

It is difficult to imagine the grim nature of Paul's circumstances in prison as he began this letter to the Philippians. While physical prison is only experienced by some, prison as a concept is universal. We have all had times when we felt "trapped" in our circumstances: a relationship, a secret, a job we dislike, a devastating medical diagnosis, dare I say in a car with a cranky child on a long road trip?! As Paul begins this letter in prison he demonstrates one of the powerful ways he worked to cultivate joy in these difficult circumstances. Paul called to mind his friends. We should note that these were not meet-and-greet acquaintances; rather, he refers to them as partners in the Gospel. These were people whom he longed for "with the affection of Christ Jesus," deep friendships developed over a time of sharing faith, hardship, victories, and intentionality of purpose. My husband refers to these types of friends in his life as those who have "spilled blood in the same mud."

What is interesting to consider here is that Paul was not a Philippian. He arrived in Philippi as a newcomer, bringing with him an unfamiliar Message for an unfamiliar people. Paul was the new guy in town. Haven't we all been there at one point? It can be hard to be the new person in school, on the job, in the meeting, on the new committee, or arriving in the new town where we don't know a soul. The experience of being new to a group is at the very least uncomfortable and for some extremely anxiety-provoking. Even though Paul was armed with God's call on his life to reach the Gentiles, I imagine that as his feet made their way along the dusty road toward Philippi, Paul may have thought, *Who will welcome me here? Who will join in this work with me? Who will be my true friend?*

While we aren't studying all of Paul's journeys here, a quick glance through his letters shows that he established a good handful of meaningful relationships many of the places he went. Thus, at some point during each of his journeys, Paul had to make the intentional choice to reach out, be vulnerable, and establish an authentic friendship or two. The first time he would have needed to find new friends was after his conversion as the old group of Pharisees were likely not on board with his new goals. Then, again, each and every time he moved to a new city to reach new people, Paul would seek new relationships.

Paul was able to cultivate joy by calling on the memories of these significant relationships because he was willing to make them in the first place.

God's words to us today are a challenge of how we think about and do relationships. It is a vulnerable thing to be authentic with others, to put ourselves out there in ministry or in the day-to-day challenge it is to live for Christ. It can be hard to tell people we are hurting, that we feel trapped, or that we want to take a risk and try something new. However, it is even harder to do life alone, and it is also not how we were designed. Paul encourages us to pursue real relationships, the kind of relationships that bring us joy when we are trapped in our prisons.

I don't know how Paul chose the people he did, but I would offer one final caveat as we begin to think about those who may become these kinds of friends for us. In between his statements of affection, he offers this statement about his friends: "he who began a good work in you will carry it on to completion until the day of Christ Jesus." I have always taken comfort in this passage, feeling the grace of God saying that we are works in progress that He intends to bring to completion. Paul is acknowledging that the people he had as friends were not finished works, they were not perfectly righteous people, nor was their work altogether finished when they parted ways. May we give God the freedom to cast a wide net for those who may become our "blood in the mud" sisters and brothers. We tend to be far more selective about people than God is. It is possible that He may have picked out someone you may have never imagined.

"Sweet Jesus, thank You for being a relational God. You did not remain distant but brought yourself as close to man as your divinity would allow. And You had friends! At least 12 really good ones! Would You cultivate joy in me today by bringing people to my mind who have been this type of friend? And in those times when I feel alone, and when these kinds of friendships are missing from my life, I ask that You would bring those people along and give me Your eyes to recognize them. I desire to know and experience authentic and intentional friendships. Grow me in this today, Lord."

Reflection Questions:

Reflect on the value that can come from intentionally pursuing deep, authentic, friendships.

_____

_____

_____

_____

_____

In contrast, what challenges me about being vulnerable and authentic with others?

_____

_____

_____

_____

_____

Share a story of someone who has been a "blood in the mud" friend, the memory of which could help carry me through a hard time now.

_____

_____

_____

_____

_____

Whom could I reach out to and begin the process of getting to know one another better or to further deepen the friendship we already have? What is one practical step I could take to do this?

_____

_____

_____

_____

_____

Day 3, *Philippians 1:9-11 (Learning)*

⁹ And this is my prayer: that your love may abound more and more in knowledge and depth of insight, ¹⁰ so that you may be able to discern what is best and may be pure and blameless for the day of Christ, ¹¹ filled with the fruit of righteousness that comes through Jesus Christ—to the glory and praise of God.

It does not take a whole lot of living to move past the romantic notion that love is only a feeling. Very often love is a verb, a choice, a decision you make to put others before yourself. Love as an action is something we regularly have to put into practice on our jobs, in our homes, as we daily go about interacting with God's people in a world that is more than just a little bit broken. However, today, Paul adds a concept to love that shifts our focus from our hearts to our minds. He tells the people of Philippi that he is praying for their love to grow specifically "in knowledge and depth of insight."

Love that is driven by emotion alone has a sense of beauty to it, but it can also feel reckless and unguided. Love that is grown in knowledge and depth of insight is more grounded; it is an informed love. The English language uses the word "love" broadly, using the same word for love of spouse, love of country, love of a great meal, or love of my new, sparkly sandals. The Greek language, however, has caveats on the word love, such as *filio*, the love of a friend, and *eros*, the love for your romantic partner. The Greek word for love that Paul is using here is *agape*. Agape is the word used for love when someone is referring to sacrificial love, the kind of love God has for us.

Paul tells us that when we grow in our knowledge of this agape love, we reap some very specific rewards. As our understanding of God's sacrificial love for us deepens, Paul suggests we become *"…able to discern what is best…be pure and blameless…filled with the fruit of righteousness that comes through Jesus Christ."* In short, growing this kind of love gives us what we need to make better, more Christ-like decisions. I'm on board for that, but how do we do it?

The way to grow our love in knowledge and depth of insight, at the risk of sounding overly simple, is to intentionally pursue knowledge and insight. We have to spend time learning about Him! Paul is offering his prayer that the Philippian people are studying, learning, and engaging in dialogue with one another to better understand who God is, so they can be more like Him. When we move our understanding of love from one of emotion to one of knowledge, we are better equipped to live for Him and love others for Him.

We can only do better when we know HIM better.

As we grow in our knowledge of Him, we can then use that information in our day-to-day experiences. We all regularly face situations in our lives when we need to be able to discern what is best. Should I change jobs? Which church should I choose? Which parenting approach is right for my children? Am I supposed to stay in this relationship? How am I supposed to handle this difficult situation at work? How should I deal with this person who is so unkind to me? I love that we serve a God who not only values our faith but also encourages us to use our minds when we are making important decisions! Pray, yes. Seek guidance from the Holy Spirit, yes. But He also wants us to be able to make knowledge-backed decisions that are pure and righteous because we have learned enough to know what that decision might be. Use the mind He gave you to make informed decisions when the need arises.

There is great joy to be found in the satisfaction of knowing that you have grown in your knowledge and love of God so much that you have confidence as you set out among the challenges of the world. Not only have you prayed and sought the internal guidance of the Holy Spirit, but you have also searched Scripture, spoken with wise and learned people who have gone before you, and maybe read a book or two if that applies. There is something to be said for the joy that can come from knowing you have made a God-informed decision. You may not be sure of what is ahead, but you know that no stone was left unturned in your approach, and you can trust God with the results. He designed you with a brain that continually develops over a lifetime. Take the time to learn about Him and refine it, so it thinks, loves, and allows you to be more like Him.

"Lord, I thank You that You value our minds and the learning process. You have given us so many resources to grow our knowledge and understanding of You so that we can in turn discern what is best. As we grow our love in this way, we will better be able to serve You, care for others, and make wise decisions that are effective and fruitful. Show me something You would like for me to learn today, Lord. I want to know and love You more."

Reflection Questions:

How might my ability to love people look different if I grow in knowledge and depth of insight?

_____

_____

_____

_____

_____

What are the typical steps I take to seek out God's guidance in a situation?

_____

_____

_____

_____

_____

What are some decisions or situations in my life where I would like to gain some discernment?

_____

_____

_____

_____

_____

What are some practical resources (books, online resources, wisdom of others) that could help me learn more about this issue?

_____

_____

_____

_____

_____

Day 4, *Philippians 1:12-14 (Eternal Perspective)*

¹²Now I want you to know, brothers and sisters, that what has happened to me has actually served to advance the gospel. ¹³As a result, it has become clear throughout the whole palace guard and to everyone else that I am in chains for Christ. ¹⁴And because of my chains, most of the brothers and sisters have become confident in the Lord and dare all the more to proclaim the gospel without fear.

When difficult or tragic things happen in life, many of us, rightly so, cling tightly to Romans 8:28: *"And we know that in all things God works for the good of those who love him, who have been called according to his purpose."* It is reassuring to read these words and be reminded that we are not outside of God's love and that He will bring good from the challenges we face. However, although far less referenced, I would suggest that the section of Philippians above runs a close second in terms of providing us support, encouragement, and perspective when faced with the "But why, God?" things of life.

It is interesting to note that the focus of Romans 8:28 is ourselves. We find comfort in knowing that God is working for *our* good. The beauty of today's verses in Philippians is that it takes the purpose of challenges beyond ourselves where we can rest in a different kind of comfort and purpose. I can say that there have been more than a few times in my life when I have needed more than Romans because I am trying to digest a Philippians type of situation.

As Paul sat in prison thinking of all that he could be doing and having no power to do so, he made this statement: *"I want you to know…what has happened to me has actually served to <u>advance the gospel</u>."* A man deeply rooted in his faith, Paul may have felt secure in God's love and purpose for him; however, I can imagine that maybe he could have begun to worry about those he was supposed to be reaching with the Gospel: the men and women he had taught in cities he visited on other journeys and the people he had yet to reach but had no idea whether or not he would ever get out of prison to do so. Philippians 1:12 is the kind of "booster" verse we need when we are set firmly in our belief that God loves us and has our best interest in mind, but we are worried about the larger fallout around a situation.

> …when we have faced an unfair firing, and we know that God has our future in His hand, but we are worried about the people and the work we are leaving behind…
>
> …when we see tragedy upon tragedy on television and wonder what good can come of it…
>
> …when we are told that the life of one of our loved ones will end too soon when there seemed so much ahead…

When we are sure in our hearts that God is good, but we have no idea why He has allowed something, I would encourage you to pray with passion that what has happened—to you, your friend, your sister, your parent, to that devastated family on the news—has the eternal purpose of advancing the Gospel. Paul cultivated joy in his situation because he was sure that this imprisonment had purpose beyond him, not just for him. His tragedy served to advance the Gospel.

The God we serve does not waste.

Isn't that what we see? When the Twin Towers came down, people returned to their faith. When a community member loses their home, people show up in droves to help. When life is lost too soon, the words offered by the dying inspire long after they are gone. God does not waste tragic situations for us personally and, maybe more so, He certainly does not waste the positive ripple effect a tragedy can create for the Kingdom. He weeps when we weep; He hurts when we hurt. While the enemy may bring pain, loss, and disease in our broken world, our God uses it not only for our good but for the advancement of the Gospel. We cultivate joy today by believing that we serve a purposeful and resourceful God who wastes no tragedy but instead utilizes it to reach others and embolden them to *"…become confident in the Lord and dare all the more to proclaim the gospel without fear."* He knows how to use everything for good. May we trust Him in this.

"Lord, I pray that You would grow my trust and understanding in the sovereignty You have over all situations. While sometimes I may get the privilege of seeing how Your hand was at work, sometimes I do not, and I am left to believe that You are guiding that situation for good. Set our minds in an eternal perspective rather than the narrow perspective of humanity. Help me today to claim my difficulties as an opportunity for You to advance the Gospel."

Reflection Questions:

What difficulty have I encountered that left me in a "But why?" state with the Lord?

_____

_____

_____

_____

_____

What situation have I been through where I now can see where God used it for my good and/or for the "advancement of the Gospel"?

_____

_____

_____

_____

_____

In my own words, write down words of comfort that I may be able to offer someone who is wondering "why" something difficult has happened.

_____

_____

_____

_____

_____

If there are areas of your life where you do not feel God has fully redeemed a difficulty or tragedy, offer that to Him in prayer today. Ask Him to show you how that has not been a "waste."

_____

_____

_____

_____

_____

Week Two

Day 5, *Philippians 1:15-18 (Keeping the Main Thing the Main Thing)*

¹⁵ It is true that some preach Christ out of envy and rivalry, but others out of goodwill. ¹⁶ The latter do so out of love, knowing that I am put here for the defense of the gospel. ¹⁷ The former preach Christ out of selfish ambition, not sincerely, supposing that they can stir up trouble for me while I am in chains. ¹⁸ But what does it matter? The important thing is that in every way, whether from false motives or true, Christ is preached. And because of this I rejoice.

Paul sets out today to tackle one of the difficult truths of working with other people in the faith. Some people are seeking to teach others about Christ out of love and goodwill. However, he also tells us that others have less pure motives and may be driven by selfish ambition, a lack of sincerity, or in hopes that they are waylaying someone else's efforts.

The truly difficult thing about the charge Paul is making is that without divine insight to see into someone's heart, we can rarely be sure of someone else's intentions. Often, when we find ourselves at odds with other Christians, it is because we don't like how they "do Jesus." In other words, we often get uncomfortable when someone else doesn't worship, speak or preach the Gospel as we do.

The Bible has its fair share of direct rules and firm no-no's. When something is happening that is clearly sinful, then it needs to be confronted. However, God also left us a whole lot of gray area in life that we are tasked to interpret via His precepts, prayer, and the wisdom of the Holy Spirit. For example, He told us many times to love people, but there is no place in Scripture that says whether that recent donation to the church should be used for missions in Uganda or ministry to the homeless down the street. He calls us to serve in our churches, but He gives no guidance on which specific person should be in charge of the children's ministry. He states that we are not supposed to give up meeting together, but He may not give you a direct answer about whether it is time to move out of the building you have been renting to build a larger space for the congregation. In short, there is a whole lot of space left where we may be wondering about the motives of the people around us or questioning our own.

Paul acknowledges that people sometimes struggle with self-driven motives while they are simultaneously trying to "preach Christ." As we consider this idea further, it really isn't that surprising at all. We are a fallen people trying our level best to live for Jesus and reach others for Him. We tend to become more self-focused when we get tired or lonely, when finances are at stake, when change is imposed, and when we are stretched thin in our commitments. We continue to try to live for Christ, but sometimes the decisions we make are more about our comfort rather than His love.

Sharing Christ is first and foremost about the Message, not the messenger.

Now before we go shaming ourselves (or anybody else) into a corner, the solution that Paul shares with us is incredible. While we often sit around attempting to judge the intentions of others or discern if we are being pure in our efforts for Christ, Paul does no such thing. The amazing way that he resolves this issue is that he doesn't! *"But what does it matter? The important thing is that in every way, whether from false motives or true, Christ is preached. And because of this I rejoice."* He simply acknowledges that people sometimes preach Christ from self-driven motives and says that he simply gets joy from knowing people are hearing about Jesus. As a recovering perfectionist, I want to scream, "If you are not doing it right, then don't do it at all!" Sadly, I would limit my own efforts and those of others if Christ were only shared when someone's heart was perfectly pure. Paul stated that he found joy by focusing on the fact that Christ was being preached rather than spending his time focused on how or why it was being done.

I imagine if Paul were one of my modern-day friends, with a little bit of sass verse 18 might be translated, "Don't get your britches in a bunch. As long as people are learning about Jesus, who cares why that person is sharing the Truth? You are going to be a whole lot happier if you focus on what really matters." May we have the wisdom today to focus on the accuracy of Christ's message being preached rather than the sanctity of the person doing it.

"Lord, we admit to You that ideally we would always have a pure heart when it comes to the decisions we make to try to share Your message. We also humbly acknowledge that we are sinful and broken and sometimes driven by our own needs. May You give us the grace to continue Your work out of our broken efforts and trust You to fill in the cracks. May the Truth about You come from us even when our intentions are misaligned."

Reflection Questions:

Reflect on ways Jesus is able to use His message even if it is being shared by someone who has self-focused motives.

_____

_____

_____

_____

_____

What is something that I have gotten "stuck" on when others share Christ that I could let go of? (Something that does not reduce the central message of the Gospel).

_____

_____

_____

_____

_____

Share a time when I have been living my life for Christ, but my motives were, at least somewhat, self-focused.

_____

_____

_____

_____

_____

Create a statement in your own words that you could share with others to help refocus situations on the central purpose of preaching Christ rather than peripheral concerns.

_____

_____

_____

_____

_____

Day 6, *Philippians 1:19-26 (End of Life)*

Yes, and I will continue to rejoice, ¹⁹for I know that through your prayers and God's provision of the Spirit of Jesus Christ what has happened to me will turn out for my deliverance. ²⁰I eagerly expect and hope that I will in no way be ashamed, but will have sufficient courage so that now as always Christ will be exalted in my body, whether by life or by death. ²¹For to me, to live is Christ and to die is gain. ²²If I am to go on living in the body, this will mean fruitful labor for me. Yet what shall I choose? I do not know! ²³I am torn between the two: I desire to depart and be with Christ, which is better by far; ²⁴but it is more necessary for you that I remain in the body. ²⁵Convinced of this, I know that I will remain, and I will continue with all of you for your progress and joy in the faith, ²⁶so that through my being with you again your boasting in Christ Jesus will abound on account of me.

Today we are going to take a sharp left turn toward a more somber note. We talked early on in this study about the challenge of being trapped in situations that are less than ideal and the ways that Paul coped in his own difficult circumstances. However, as he progresses in his letter today, it becomes clear that Paul is at the point where he would be content if his life were not to continue. Paul says that he is torn between the fruit that will come from continuing to live for Christ and help others versus the desire he has to leave this Earth and be with Jesus.

The truth is that most of us will face this type of tension at some point in our own lives. For many of us, it will not be until we are older, suffering with disease and the effects of the march of time. It is a time when we will do our best to honor Him in our last days, but the thought of being home with Jesus will be a welcome one. In contrast, the challenging circumstances of Paul's life placed him in this tension when he was a far younger man.

Regardless of whether you have ever felt torn between life on Earth or being home with Christ, learning how to be content with the thought of death has immense value no matter our age. Of course we all wish for long, happy lives where we get to see the fruits of our labors come to fruition. Few desire to depart before their time; however, it is essential to realize that life itself can become an idol.

Paul got ahold of this concept really well, and because of this, he was uniquely able to cultivate joy. He found joy in his challenges because he believed that Christ would be glorified whether he lived or died. He then stated, "*I am torn between the two: I desire to depart and be with Christ, which is better by far; but it is more necessary for you that I remain in the body. Convinced of this, I know that I will remain, and I will continue with all of you for your progress and joy in the faith…*" He knew God would keep him around for a while because it was better for the people he was serving. He recognized that he had work to do but declared his life mattered little compared to being with Christ. "*For to me, to live is Christ and to die is gain."* In short, Paul was okay with living as God called him to and dying when God said it was time.

Reflecting on eternity with Christ is a powerful antidote for fear.

Consider the freedom that may come in our lives if our perspective became that of Paul. If we went through each day trusting and knowing that God will keep us here exactly as long as He needs to for the people we are supposed to "progress in the faith" while simultaneously looking forward to the day He calls us Home because we believe to *"be with Christ…is better by far."* How many of us have lost sleep worrying about the possibility of leaving "too soon," of what would happen to our children, our spouse, our parents, our life's work? Moreover, how many times have we rented way too much space in our heads to the fear of losing loved ones, getting a knock on the door after an accident, or wondering if that slight twitch we felt might be something much more serious?

Paul's example does not ask us to hope for death to arrive before its time; he is simply acknowledging the joy that comes from knowing that it will be purposeful. He does not fear the end of life because he knows that he will not leave before he is supposed to, and when he does leave, he gets to be with Jesus. He has prioritized his life below Christ, not just in practice but in its very existence. The concept of letting go of the value we place on our lives initially sounds terrifying, but the reality is that there is great joy in being free of the fear of the end. Rather than worrying about the end, it is our job to live daily for Christ, trust in His timing and care for those things that are so valuable to us, and cultivate the joy that comes from the thought of sitting with Him someday.

"Lord, we really fear death sometimes. We fear our own end, but often more we fear the end of life for those we love. Sometimes these types of worries take up so much of our time and energy that they have become an idol we are seeking to preserve at all costs, taking away from our living for You. May You help us to release our stranglehold on life today and bring us the security and joy that comes from trusting You with the entirety of our lives, from beginning to end. May our ultimate destination with You always feel like a 'gain.'"

Reflection Questions:

How have my experiences with loss of life shaped how I understand death?

_____

_____

_____

_____

_____

What emotions does eternity with Christ bring about for me?

_____

_____

_____

_____

_____

What are the fears that keep me from embracing the thought of heaven being a "gain"?

_____

_____

_____

_____

_____

What work do I have on this Earth that I am excited to do in my time of "fruitfulness"?

_____

_____

_____

_____

_____

Day 7, *Philippians 1:27-30 (Integrity)*

²⁷ Whatever happens, conduct yourselves in a manner worthy of the gospel of Christ. Then, whether I come and see you or only hear about you in my absence, I will know that you stand firm in the one Spirit, striving together as one for the faith of the gospel ²⁸ without being frightened in any way by those who oppose you. This is a sign to them that they will be destroyed, but that you will be saved—and that by God. ²⁹ For it has been granted to you on behalf of Christ not only to believe in him, but also to suffer for him, ³⁰ since you are going through the same struggle you saw I had, and now hear that I still have.

Early in my training as a therapist I was taught to lead people away from extremes, particularly in family or couples counseling. Phrases like "You *always* do this" or "You *never* do that" are often particularly counterproductive when attempting to resolve interpersonal issues. However, there are a handful of times when God pulls out the big guns and gives us an "always" or a "never" where there is no wiggle room. Verse 27 offers us this kind of challenge. *"Whatever happens, conduct yourselves in a manner worthy of the gospel of Christ." Whatever* happens?! Yes, whatever happens.

As people we tend to attach asterisks to situations. We know God calls us to react in ways that honor Him, but sometimes it seems a situation is just too much, and we choose a different response. Our bent toward it starts early. "He pushed me first" and "But I didn't get a turn" turn into "But I did the work. Why didn't I get the promotion?" and "They cut me off! $%&#^%&!" Responding to situations in a Christ-like way *no matter what* isn't generally a problem when things are going well. However, when we start wandering into the realm of those things that are unfair, unjust, unkind, or straight up wrong it becomes much harder.

Now, before you shut the book today with the awful taste of legalism in your mouth, think back to a concept we talked about on day three: learning, increasing our love with knowledge. Verse 27 says, *"…conduct yourselves in a manner worthy of the gospel of Christ."* It does not say, "Keep your mouth shut all the time," "Let people walk all over you," or "Have a really nice, pleasant tone and say, 'Bless your heart.'"

Christ is our ultimate example for how to act in a manner worthy of the Gospel, and His responses covered a wide range of actions and emotions. When things got intense, sometimes He got really upset, or called people out, or full on asked for a way out of His calling in the Garden of Gethsemane. However, He also sometimes said nothing, told a story instead of confronting someone directly, or just sweepingly pardoned the whole of humanity with His sacrifice. The thing that let Him respond perfectly in every situation was that He made every decision out of a knowledge-filled love.

We are far more likely to choose the "right" reaction when our driving force is love.

He was able to discern that the most loving thing for the woman in adultery was to initially call upon the hypocrisy of her accusers (John 8). It was love that let him decide to flip a few tables in the temple rather than have a quiet side conversation with the merchants (Matthew 21:12). It was also love that led Him to acknowledge the bleeding woman's faith rather than her stigmatized condition (Mark 5). It was love that led Him to the cross rather than enforcing the consequences of our sin on our own lives.

It is our job to seek out how to "conduct ourselves in a manner worthy of the gospel of Christ." We do not have the option of conditional morality, but we do have the example of Christ in every situation we encounter. He did nothing impulsively and everything from a position of considering others in love. As challenges greet us today, may we feel the permission to pause before we react and seek God's guidance on how to "conduct ourselves." Operating in this way cultivates joy by letting us be in congruence with Christ and responding out of love. And, when we stumble, we can call on Him again to help us be better informed and driven by love the next time around.

Lord, help me today to conduct myself in a manner worthy of Your Gospel. Even more, teach me! You have shown me in Your Word that acting in love does not always look the same, but I need an extra dose of the Holy Spirit to know what I am supposed to do in situations when I have been hurt or mistreated or when the guidelines are unclear. Help me to lead a thoughtful life where I pause before I react to difficult situations so that You can instruct me as I move forward. May I seek to do this to cultivate my own joy through consistent behavior and bless others with it as well."

Reflection Questions:

What are some areas of my life where I have a hard time reacting in a Christ-like way?

_____

_____

_____

_____

_____

What are some examples Jesus gave us in the Bible that may help me better know how to handle these situations?

_____

_____

_____

_____

_____

Reflect on ways I (or others) may benefit from my growth in Christ-centered humility.

_____

_____

_____

_____

_____

Create a short prayer that will help me to pause and center myself before I act in situations.

_____

_____

_____

_____

_____

Day 8, *Philippians 2:3-8 (Christ-Centered Identity)*

Therefore if you have any encouragement from being united with Christ, if any comfort from his love, if any common sharing in the Spirit, if any tenderness and compassion, [2] then make my joy complete by being like-minded, having the same love, being one in spirit and of one mind. Do nothing out of selfish ambition or vain conceit. Rather, in humility value others above yourselves, [4] not looking to your own interests but each of you to the interests of the others. [5] In your relationships with one another, have the same mindset as Christ Jesus: [6] Who, being in very nature God, did not consider equality with God something to be used to his own advantage; [7] rather, he made himself nothing by taking the very nature of a servant, being made in human likeness. [8] And being found in appearance as a man, he humbled himself by becoming obedient to death—even death on a cross!

One of the things we can really appreciate about Paul is that he "got his hands dirty." This man who is calling us to live out the challenging ideas and behaviors listed in Philippians did not lead some sort of idyllic, comfortable life. While his early life may have been one with resources, prestige, and power, his conversion on the road to Damascus changed his life and lifestyle dramatically. It must have been quite the switch for him to go from being a Pharisee persecuting the early Christians to a renegade disciple of Christ. Rather than living in the posh limelight of religiosity, he was now traveling thousands of miles, enduring hardship, physical ailments, beatings, prison, mocking, and disdain as he shared the fledgling message of Christianity. The entire experience may have been extremely humbling as he was "taken down a few pegs" among the people who had power and privilege. Paul knew what it was like to live life thinking he was a big deal and then coming to the realization that he was not. This is the kind of person we can get behind when he starts sharing some thoughts on service and humility.

In the verses today, Paul takes a step away from talking about his own experiences and shines the light directly on the person of Christ. He begins by calling on us to do nothing that is selfishly driven or motivated by our own vanity. He then goes further to suggest that in addition to not being driven by our own wants, we should value other people above ourselves and pay attention to what other people need. Eek! As a therapist I always start to twitch a little when I read these words because it sounds like a breeding ground for poor self-care and an open door for selfish and abusive people to take advantage. So what are we to do with the example of Christ's servanthood as we attempt to live it out in our own lives? We look at the whole of His example.

A Christ-centered identity marries humility and value and produces the offspring of love and service.

While not listed in these verses, as we look at Christ's life we see times when He rested, He took time with friends, He spent time learning and in church, He had time in solitude and time alone in prayer, He ate and He traveled, He asked His disciples to pray for Him, He even napped! The difference between us and Christ is that His motivation for self-care or "self-indulgent" activity was always pure and intentional because His needs and identity were already perfectly met in God alone. When Christ rested and ate, he likely enjoyed it, but it was intended as fuel for the ministry He would do later. When He traveled, He probably enjoyed the time with His friends, but He always maintained his focus on loving and serving people along the way. He took time away from others in solitude and prayer. In His alone time with His Father, which was hopefully intensely satisfying, the byproduct was refreshment for the service and ministry ahead.

Today's verses about humility and service are not a call to decide that we have no value. On the contrary! Jesus never decided He wasn't valuable or that He didn't have needs. The difference between us and Jesus is that He realized His needs and value were met in God alone. He gives us the example of finding our value in Whose we are rather than who we are to free us from striving to establish our value on our own. When we are not spending our time fighting to establish our own importance, then we have the freedom to spend our energy loving others. When we are trusting God with meeting our needs rather than feeling like we have to scramble for scraps, then we are free to serve others with our time and our resources. When we go through our days filled with the truth that we are God's kid, we are going to have far more of ourselves to give away in the service and love of others. When we are filled with the truth of who we are in Christ, then we can be humble knowing that we are not that big of a deal, but we are a big deal to God. It is out of His love that we can then value the needs and interest of others above our own because He has already met ours in Jesus.

"Jesus, it is a really tricky thing to find the entirety of our value in You when we have so many other identities we can hold. Help us to know when we are being self-indulgent and when we are being God-indulgent. Give us the wisdom to pattern our lives after Your service, love, and humility without allowing ourselves to step away from finding our significance in You. Fill us with joy as we are able to love and serve Your people out of an overflow of Your love for us."

Reflection Questions:

What are the main things that I find my identity in?

_____

_____

_____

_____

_____

What are some areas where I feel that I am fighting for significance?

_____

_____

_____

_____

_____

How could I give those needs over to God and be better satisfied in Him alone?

_____

_____

_____

_____

_____

Reflect on a day when my identity and needs are found solely in God. How could that better enable me to love and serve others?

_____

_____

_____

_____

_____

Week Three

Day 9, *Philippians 2:12-13 (Giving Up Perfection & Control)*

12 Therefore, my dear friends, as you have always obeyed—not only in my presence, but now much more in my absence—continue to work out your salvation with fear and trembling, 13 for it is God who works in you to will and to act in order to fulfill his good purpose.

I suspect there are many things I may have accomplished by now had I been able to quiet the "But what will happen?" perfectionist/controlling section of my brain. We all have talents, gifts, and callings in our lives, but it is hard to embrace them and strike out not knowing how it will all turn out. A great deal of what keeps us from moving forward in God's calling is fear. Fear of whether or not we have what it takes, fear of "failure," fear of what others may think, fear of what may happen to the current state of our lives, fear of the unknown. We fear a lot of things that we are not supposed to and forget to fear the One we are supposed to, God himself. Today we'll look at a couple of verses outside of Philippians that reference the fear of the Lord:

"Blessed are those who fear the Lord, who find great delight in His commands." Psalm 112:1

"The fear of the Lord is the beginning of wisdom and knowledge of the Holy One is understanding." Proverbs 9:10

"The fear of the Lord is the beginning of knowledge but fools despise wisdom and instruction." Proverbs 1:7

"The fear of the Lord is a fountain of life, turning a person away from the snares of death." Proverbs 14:27

"In the fear of the Lord one has strong confidence, and his children will have a refuge." Proverbs 14:26 (ESV)

"The friendship of the Lord is for those who fear him, and he makes known to them his covenant." Psalm 25:14 (ESV)

I don't know about you, but fear of things other than the Lord has not typically had the positive consequences suggested in the verses above. Fear of things of the world tends to create paralysis of motivation; missed opportunities; emotional, mental and physical discomfort; and giving power to something or someone who does not deserve it. The fear of the Lord, however, is the reverential fear of Someone who loves us and has our best interest in mind. It is a fear based on the recognition of His total power and authority in our lives and our necessary dependence on Him each day. It is a fear that results in the "consequences" we see above: blessing, the beginning of wisdom, the beginning of knowledge, a fountain of life that protects us, confidence, refuge for our children, and my favorite…friendship with the Lord. Frankly, that's the kind of fear I'd like to have!

Fear of the Lord is an antidote for any other anxiety.

Now that we have figured out who is the One to yield our fears to, we can really settle in to the second half of these verses. Paul tells us in verse 13 that it is God who works *in you*. Do you participate? Sure. Are you more than just a puppet with strings? Of course! But are we occasionally hampering God's work at times with our own stranglehold on controlling things? Probably. We often have our own ideas about how we want things to go. We poke and prod at situations trying to force them into a nice, neat, bow-adorned end. Paul offers us a breath of freedom from this micromanagement in the final words of verse 13 stating, *"...for it is God who works in you to will and to act in order to fulfill his good purpose."* If Paul were sassy, we might have heard that another way: "It ain't about you!" God loves us, and He more than once mentions that He loves doing good things for us and with us! However, ultimately it is all about Him, and we get to play our part in that great big moving picture of Him redeeming His people. When we are able to shift our focus toward "His good purpose" rather than manhandling the results out of fear, then the perspective we have changes:

If He calls me to write a book, and I don't worry about if I'll sound smart enough but instead focus on the people He intends to reach, I'll be more likely to start typing.

If He tells me to reach out to that community who breaks my heart, and I focus on whom He wants to reach rather than how it may affect my pocketbook, I'll be more likely to follow through.

If He challenges me to a new career, and I focus on how I will bring His light to my new coworkers rather than whether I will be "good at it," I'll be more likely to apply.

Be brave, my friend, and move forward knowing that the only Fear you need has already overcome any fear you may have.

"Lord Jesus, may you help me today to set aside what I fear, so I can think about what You want. Push away fears I have of things in the world and those that are rooted in my own insecurities. Make me brave because You are working in me, and that is all I need. Give me joy today as I do Your work, and help me leave the results and consequences to You."

Reflection Questions:

What are the fears that bother me the most in my life?

_____

_____

_____

_____

_____

What is something I have always wanted to do but have been too scared/worried to move forward?

_____

_____

_____

_____

_____

What is one small step I can take toward trusting Him in this desire and moving forward?

_____

_____

_____

_____

_____

Whom do I have in my life that I could help support in something he/she has been called to do but may have been too fearful to move forward?

_____

_____

_____

_____

_____

Day 10, Philippians 2:14-18 (Positive Attitude)

¹⁴ Do everything without grumbling or arguing, ¹⁵ so that you may become blameless and pure, "children of God without fault in a warped and crooked generation." Then you will shine among them like stars in the sky ¹⁶ as you hold firmly to the word of life. And then I will be able to boast on the day of Christ that I did not run or labor in vain. ¹⁷ But even if I am being poured out like a drink offering on the sacrifice and service coming from your faith, I am glad and rejoice with all of you. ¹⁸ So you too should be glad and rejoice with me.

Maintaining a positive attitude in our current culture is no easy task. While past generations certainly had access to negativity, at least they had to work a little bit harder than we do to hear it. The news only came through on regularly scheduled programming, people voiced their opinions via editorials in the (print) newspaper delivered once a day, or the nosy neighbor next door offered his or her opinion on what "should" be happening in the community. On the contrary, today we are offered the opportunity to read anyone's unfiltered (and often anonymous) opinion on news or social media available to us around the clock. We have texting, e-mail, social media, online news outlets, blogs, and forums that allow us to engage with the opinions of others ad nauseam. Likewise, we are also able to offer our unfiltered and possibly anonymous opinion to the world without any check on our own motivation or intention. A perceived lack of accountability is a great temptation to set our values aside.

In addition to the choices we make from behind a screen, we of course have face-to-face interactions with others every day. We have the choice whether to join in and stoke the fires of our disgruntled coworkers, offer criticisms of our children's teachers and coaches, or have "roast pastor" each Sunday at lunch. Our children take notice of how we process the challenging things that happen to us, how we talk about the work that needs to get done, and if we speak about people differently when they are around than when they are absent.

Whether digitally or in person, engaging in positivity or negativity is a pattern that often becomes a habit. To be clear, Jesus does not call us to be inauthentic, pretending that things are okay when they are not. However, when addressing concerns, He does call us to "speak the truth in love" (Eph. 4:15). Speaking the truth in love has an end goal of bringing a person, a group, or a situation more in line with Christ's values. On the other hand, "grumbling and arguing" is usually self-focused, judgmental, and utilized to help us feel justified or alleviate some discomfort. There is a stark difference between being real and being negative.

Negativity begets negativity. Positivity begets positivity.

So why does having a positive mindset matter? Our effectiveness for Christ as well as our internal experience of joy is directly affected by what we ingest and what we express. Maybe even more importantly, Paul shares with us today that if we can live our lives without a pattern of arguing and complaining, we will "shine among them like stars in the sky." In short, we are going to stand out! And this standing out is not about ourselves; instead it is about being an example of Christ's love to those whom we encounter. We are going to stand out because our world is deeply broken. As Paul says above, we are "in a warped and crooked generation." There are really awful things that happen to us or around us all the time, and we will be beacons of light if we are able to maintain a positive, joyful attitude in the midst of all the mess.

Today our goal is to begin shifting away from negativity in the information we take in and the words and behaviors that we express. Just as with our physical health, we are what we eat mentally, emotionally, and spiritually. May you be blessed today as you pursue a positive attitude that sets you apart from the pattern of the world.

"Lord Jesus, it is so easy to join in with the discontentment of the world. In fact, sometimes it feels like it helps when we feel lonely, hurt, or justified in some wrong. Help us to find joy in You today so that our happenings do not determine our happiness. Refine our practices and our patterns away from arguing and complaining so that we can better represent You in a world that loves to criticize. Train our eyes and our ears to see what is good."

Reflection Questions:

What do I engage with (media, friends, etc.) that feeds negativity into my life?

_____

_____

_____

_____

_____

What do I engage with that feeds positivity into my life?

_____

_____

_____

_____

_____

In what situations am I most likely to have difficulty remaining positive and instead complain and argue?

_____

_____

_____

_____

_____

What practical steps can I take today to begin ingesting and expressing more Christ-like attitudes?

_____

_____

_____

_____

_____

Day 11, *Philippians 2:19-30 (Diversity and Intentionality of Relationship)*

19 I hope in the Lord Jesus to send Timothy to you soon, that I also may be cheered when I receive news about you. 20 I have no one else like him, who will show genuine concern for your welfare. 21 For everyone looks out for their own interests, not those of Jesus Christ. 22 But you know that Timothy has proved himself, because as a son with his father he has served with me in the work of the gospel. 23 I hope, therefore, to send him as soon as I see how things go with me. 24 And I am confident in the Lord that I myself will come soon.

25 But I think it is necessary to send back to you Epaphroditus, my brother, co-worker and fellow soldier, who is also your messenger, whom you sent to take care of my needs. 26 For he longs for all of you and is distressed because you heard he was ill. 27 Indeed he was ill, and almost died. But God had mercy on him, and not on him only but also on me, to spare me sorrow upon sorrow. 28 Therefore I am all the more eager to send him, so that when you see him again you may be glad and I may have less anxiety. 29 So then, welcome him in the Lord with great joy, and honor people like him, 30 because he almost died for the work of Christ. He risked his life to make up for the help you yourselves could not give me.

Today Paul gets uniquely personal with us, sharing with us some details about a couple significant relationships in his life. Much has been said about Paul's mentoring relationship with the young Timothy, which is detailed significantly further in 1 and 2 Timothy. However, he only mentions Epaphroditus in these verses and then briefly again in the fourth chapter of Philippians. We explored early in this study the essential nature of friendship and the importance of being willing to engage in vulnerable, authentic relationships with trusted others. Today Paul gets more specific and attends to the diversity in his friendships from which we can glean some important concepts.

There is an important generational ripple effect that runs throughout Scripture as people grow in their faith: being mentored by others, mentoring those who are younger, and finding true brothers and sisters in the Lord. It is clear from Scripture and from historical record that Timothy was younger than Paul and that they operated in a Father-son type of relationship while doing ministry together. Paul's affection for Timothy is an encouragement for us to pursue these types of relationships and experience the joy that comes from watching someone grow and become what Christ has called them to be.

The second person Paul mentions above is Epaphroditus. Unlike Timothy, Epaphroditus was likely older than or about the same age as Paul. The important part to note is that Epaphroditus was a "seasoned" person in the faith. He calls him his "brother, co-worker and fellow soldier," indicating that they had been doing the hard work of life together. Paul highlights here the value of having people in our lives who have been walking in the faith, who have been through hard times, and who may have a few gray hairs to prove it.

The energy of youth and the wisdom of age make for a beautiful friendship.

Diversifying our relationship portfolio can be an effective part of cultivating joy in our lives. There is a unique kind of joy to be had from lending your time, wisdom, and experience to another to help them grow and yet another that comes from having someone do that with us. If your life is lacking in either of these categories, as many of ours are, I would encourage you to pray and seek whom God may have for you to mentor. What He has taught you thus far in your life could be immensely valuable to some young person who is seeking out the way to live for Him. Additionally, if you are without a contemporary who keeps pace with you or a seasoned veteran who can challenge your inexperience and comfort your unknowns, ask the Lord to fill these spaces. Participating in the top-down investment of God's people is a satisfying give-and-take that blesses you, your mentors, and your mentees who will then pour into the next generation.

"Lord, may my eyes be enlightened to those whom You have purposed for me to encourage in their faith as well as those who could challenge me and accompany me in mine. I will not benefit from being with only people like me. May I cultivate joy today by considering the intentional way You design your people to generationally pour Your love into one another."

Reflection Questions:

Who has mentored me in my faith, and how has that blessed me?

_____

_____

_____

_____

_____

What specific life experience or understanding do I have to share that may be a gift to someone else?

_____

_____

_____

_____

_____

Who is on my short list of people to pursue who may allow me to "diversify my friendship portfolio"?

_____

_____

_____

_____

_____

What type of generational legacy do I want to leave? What steps do I need to take to intentionally pass that on to others?

_____

_____

_____

_____

_____

Day 12, *Philippians 3:1 (Contentment in Monotony)*

Further, my brothers and sisters, rejoice in the Lord! It is no trouble for me to write the same things to you again, and it is a safeguard for you.

Today we will take a look at a single verse in Philippians that explores a powerful truth about cultivating joy. We live in a media culture that relentlessly uses comparison to romance us. Advertisements line our highways and pop up on e-mail suggesting that there is something we "need." Our Pinterest boards are filled with dreams that are sometimes far beyond our income, our time, or our talents. We are tempted to "keep up with the Joneses" or, at the very least, keep our kids up with the Joneses' kids. Interpersonally our marriages are under assault from the pressure that there should be passion and longing present every moment like the relationships we see in movies.

The world suggests that true contentment is just around the bend of another experience, another purchase, or another accomplishment. And so we bite again, grossly overestimating the happiness that will come only to find ourselves all too soon longing for the next. It is an exhausting standard to pursue, and it is one that God never intended for us to chase. There is a lot of messaging aimed at convincing us that our lives are not "enough." It is not surprising then that we sometimes experience great sadness or longing when we are spending time in the categorically monotonous, repetitious, or steady parts of our lives.

One of my favorite sections of Scripture initially sounds like a major bummer of a message about life and marriage. It makes me giggle every time because it sounds so very pitiful. An aged and experienced Solomon offers these words in Ecclesiastes 9:9: *"Enjoy life with your wife, whom you love, all the days of this meaningless life that God has given you under the sun—all your meaningless days. For this is your lot in life and in your toilsome labor under the sun."* Bahaha! It seems like such an awful downer of a statement; you can almost hear the "whah whah" noise. However, as with all of God's words, there is great wisdom to be gleaned from this idea. Our life is not supposed to have fireworks all the time; in fact, joy is found by embracing our many common and unremarkable days.

Rare is the man who finds contentment in the monotony of days, but great is his joy.

Paul's verse above alludes to a very similar sentiment. He notes that in this letter to the Philippians he is happily repeating many of the same things he has told them before. *"It is no trouble for me to write the same things to you again, and it is a safeguard for you."* Repetition is a safeguard. God did not give us "meaningless days" and the instruction to study His words over and over again to bore us. He did it because He knows how fickle we are! He knows that true joy comes from Him alone, and thus it is in love that He gives us plenty of times when our lives are not filled with the addictive presence of newness and adrenaline. He wisely designed us to need regular patterns of sleep, and food, and all those chores that keep our homes attended to. He wisely gives us counsel on how to keep our finances in check and invest in our relationships because He knows how easily we can become unfocused chasing the next best thing. The many repetitive and "boring" elements of our lives— when embraced with contentment—are a "safeguard" in this life that is filled with allure. While it is certainly okay to hope and pray for Godly changes and additional blessing in your life, imagine the joy of being content with the life *God* has given you rather than worshiping the life *you* want. When the longing for what could be is drowned out by contentment in the "now," we then have the perspective in place to cultivate joy in repetition.

"Lord, I pray that you would help me to not only find joy, but also protection from coveting as I learn to celebrate the mundane and habitual parts of my life. Bring to my mind those things that I do on a regular basis that contribute to my stability in You and also provide a steadfast, consistent blessing for others. Help me to find joy in 'the same things again' that are from You, so that I may enjoy my life in these 'meaningless days.' One of the greatest gifts You give us is that You are 'the same yesterday, today, and forever.' Let us find joy and contentment in Your example."

Reflection Questions:

What is it that I desire that distracts me from being content with the life I have?

_____

_____

_____

_____

_____

What are some habitual, consistent practices that I do that contribute positively to my own life or the life of others?

_____

_____

_____

_____

_____

What is something I do regularly in my life that I know is positive and healthy, but I am having trouble finding joy in it?

_____

_____

_____

_____

_____

What is one thing I can do to help myself be more content with the life God has given me?

_____

_____

_____

_____

_____

Week Four

Day 13, *Philippians 3:2-11 (Grasping Grace)*

² Watch out for those dogs, those evildoers, those mutilators of the flesh. ³ For it is we who are the circumcision, we who serve God by his Spirit, who boast in Christ Jesus, and who put no confidence in the flesh— ⁴ though I myself have reasons for such confidence.

If someone else thinks they have reasons to put confidence in the flesh, I have more: ⁵ circumcised on the eighth day, of the people of Israel, of the tribe of Benjamin, a Hebrew of Hebrews; in regard to the law, a Pharisee; ⁶ as for zeal, persecuting the church; as for righteousness based on the law, faultless.

⁷ But whatever were gains to me I now consider loss for the sake of Christ. ⁸ What is more, I consider everything a loss because of the surpassing worth of knowing Christ Jesus my Lord, for whose sake I have lost all things. I consider them garbage, that I may gain Christ ⁹ and be found in him, not having a righteousness of my own that comes from the law, but that which is through faith in Christ—the righteousness that comes from God on the basis of faith. ¹⁰ I want to know Christ—yes, to know the power of his resurrection and participation in his sufferings, becoming like him in his death, ¹¹ and so, somehow, attaining to the resurrection from the dead.

Paul's bluntness of speech has offended more than a few people as he is never a mincer of words and always truthful to a fault. While hopefully not being irreverent, I find the candid nature of his counsel both refreshing and amusing. He begins these verses by repeating some concepts he has shared before. He reminds us that we are a people who are set apart by our relationship with Christ. He repeats the idea that we serve God most effectively when we operate out of His spirit rather than out of our own abilities. Yes, we have seen these ideas before. But then, just in case we were still hanging on to any shred of hope that we may have something that gives us extra spiritual collateral, Paul offers us his spiritual resume.

"If someone else thinks they have reasons to put confidence in the flesh, I have more." A very informal translation of verses 5 and 6 might read, "I have way more reasons to think God would value me based on who I am. I'm one of His chosen Jewish people, a descendant straight out of the 12 tribes of Israel. I know more about the Bible than you could ever hope to know, I have passion coming out my ears, and I got straight A's in Jewish law. Beat that!" At times it is easy to see why Paul struggles with the historical bad rap of being arrogant.

While his "boasting" may initially seem egotistical, it has an important purpose. God knew we would need an example of someone who, frankly, did have a lot to offer that was his own. If someone was going to tell us that everything he has now feels like "garbage" compared to knowing Christ, it needed to be someone who really had something to lose. Because of our propensity for comparing our lives to others, God knew this message would have to come from someone who kicks our tails in credentials.

As we work to re-understand the things we value, it is important to notice that God did not take all of Paul's identifiers away. The things Paul shared in his resume were still true; he is just telling us that he has drastically reprioritized them. This call to consider all things a "loss" or "garbage" is not necessarily a command to throw all those things out. Rather, it is a shifting of our hearts toward understanding how little everything else matters in comparison to knowing Jesus and being in relationship with Him. Paul's listing of purebred awesomeness followed by his denunciation of how little those things matter is a powerful example we can learn from.

Adding our own merit to salvation is a weight we were not designed to carry.

We all benefit by taking stock of our identifiers and filtering them through a "gut check" to determine if we think those give us a "leg up" with God. We are able to cultivate such incredible joy when we are refocused on our value being found totally and completely in our identification as God's child. Anything we do that is of ourselves, no matter how talented we are, is going to fail at times. We will all make mistakes, drop the ball, or not live up to our "potential" at times. If our identity is found in our own abilities, the fall from that pedestal can be very painful. However, if we keep the value of our abilities where they belong, the landing on God's pillow of grace is far more manageable.

"Lord, I pray that today you would open my eyes to anything I think makes me more valuable to You. Free me of the weight of earning my salvation. Help me to understand that being in You is enough and that anything else leads to comparison...comparison of me to myself, of me to others, of jockeying with trinkets for Your love. Your love is a free gift given by grace alone. Help me to sit peacefully in that today."

Reflection Questions:

Reflect on Paul's spiritual resume. What do you think it was like for him to realize that all those things were "garbage"?

_____

_____

_____

_____

_____

What things do I have on my own spiritual resume that lure me into thinking they give me a "leg up" with God?

_____

_____

_____

_____

_____

How can I go about recognizing that I am saved by grace alone (Ephesians 2:8-9) while continuing to maximize the gifts He has given me?

_____

_____

_____

_____

_____

In what ways have I been trying to "earn" God's love that I can let go of today?

_____

_____

_____

_____

_____

Day 14, *Philippians 3:12-16 (Hope vs. Future Tripping)*

12 Not that I have already obtained all this, or have already arrived at my goal, but I press on to take hold of that for which Christ Jesus took hold of me. 13 Brothers and sisters, I do not consider myself yet to have taken hold of it. But one thing I do: Forgetting what is behind and straining toward what is ahead, 14 I press on toward the goal to win the prize for which God has called me heavenward in Christ Jesus.

15 All of us, then, who are mature should take such a view of things. And if on some point you think differently, that too God will make clear to you. 16 Only let us live up to what we have already attained.

One of the most powerful things we can do when we are studying Scripture is to consider the context of the passage we are reading. In this case, yesterday Paul called us to the big task of grasping that nothing is that big of a deal compared to knowing Jesus and that we can't earn spiritual points with our talents. When we left off, Paul was sounding pretty confident about this whole being a Christian thing and suggested we should follow suit. Well, as much as I can appreciate being challenged, I love a little bit of relatability as well. Paul gives that to us in spades today.

Today's verses are those of a man humbly acknowledging that he is on a journey with Christ, and he has not yet reached his destination. Call to mind something you have been wanting to do (or stop doing) for a long time. For many of us the emotion that follows is one of frustration or embarrassment. We think about the weeks, months, or years that have gone by without reaching that goal and feel as though we may never do it. God knows that one of the most effective ways to drain joy from our lives is for us to lose hope and adopt the fear that things cannot be different or that we cannot change. Because of this, He graciously gives us the example of Paul who admits that even he has not accomplished everything he has been called to do. While I appreciate this humble admission, the important part is what Paul says next. Rather than sitting in the shame of unrealized goals or quitting because he may never get there, he instead makes several statements of hope.

To retrieve his forward-thinking motivation, Paul reminds himself that God has "taken hold of him" for a purpose. He shifts his mindset by "forgetting what is behind and straining toward what is ahead." He talks about his goal as a "when" rather than an "if." Imagine how our attitudes toward progress and motivation would be different if we were to face each day with these same mindsets. Paul knew that in order to grow in his work and relationship with Christ, he was going to have to put the past behind him. Likewise, we have to be able to put bad days, ineffective decisions, frustrations of effort, and lapses of commitment behind us if we are ever to move forward in our goals.

If you allow your past to dictate your present, the future is unlikely to change.

In the middle of battling to win over our own perspectives, we are also battling an enemy who does not want us to be successful. One of Satan's greatest tricks is to convince us that our efforts are not worth it and that we are not capable. When given to this type of thinking we begin "future tripping" over the fear that we will continue to make the same mistakes, encounter the same realities with no change in our mindset, or never develop the skills to accomplish the goals we feel God has given us. "But I just feel so defeated sometimes. How am I supposed to start thinking this way when fighting off doubts and insecurities is a daily battle?" Thankfully Paul offers us a strategy for this concern.

Verse 15 may be one of my favorite, and grace-filled, verses in Philippians. *"All of us, then, who are mature should take such a view of things. And if on some point you think differently, that too God will make clear to you."* Initially it seems like Paul is calling us out, "Hey, if you were really mature then you would think like this." However, he provides a solution rooted in God's wisdom for us to lean on heavily, prayerfully, daily for those things that we have a hard time thinking "hopefully" about. God doesn't want us to lose hope, and He definitely does not want to leave us in the dark just for spite. Paul tells us here that we can call on His promise to make things clear to us if we are thinking "differently." Oh, how many times have I been thinking about something in one way, and then God comes in and clears up the cobwebs. And His way of thinking makes so much more sense! May He mature us so that we can have joy in the hope of our future selves as we walk alongside Paul who also knew what it meant to be "partway there."

"Jesus, sometimes I let what has happened in the past keep me from hoping and being joyful about my future. I 'trip' over thoughts of what could be rather than trusting and hoping in You. Give me a new confidence in You today and help me to believe in the truth that You have goals You have called me to. If there are ways I am thinking 'differently' than I ought, I claim Your promise to make that clear to me. Mature my views so that I am able to live more effectively for You."

Reflection Questions:

Reflect on the idea that even Paul recognized that he was an unfinished work in progress.

_____

_____

_____

_____

_____

What are the main doubts that keep me from feeling motivated and purpose-driven at times?

_____

_____

_____

_____

_____

What is something in my life that I would like to feel more confident in or sure of my abilities?

_____

_____

_____

_____

_____

Offer a personal prayer here for God to inject hope in your thinking about something that feels unchangeable to you.

_____

_____

_____

_____

_____

Day 15, *Philippians 3:17-21 (Awareness of Sin)*

[17] Join together in following my example, brothers and sisters, and just as you have us as a model, keep your eyes on those who live as we do. [18] For, as I have often told you before and now tell you again even with tears, many live as enemies of the cross of Christ. [19] Their destiny is destruction, their god is their stomach, and their glory is in their shame. Their mind is set on earthly things.[20] But our citizenship is in heaven. And we eagerly await a Savior from there, the Lord Jesus Christ, [21] who, by the power that enables him to bring everything under his control, will transform our lowly bodies so that they will be like his glorious body.

Today's lesson is going to seem like a paradox, but every single time I type that word I remember that a great many things about Jesus are a paradox. He died so we may live. He lived as a man even though He is God. He uplifts the lowly and humbles the proud. Our God is all about things that seem to be contradictory but are in fact perfect complements. God likes to make sense of things that seem upside down.

I think the message Paul shares with us in these verses today is one of the most difficult concepts we ever have to adjust to in life. Each of us has times we can think of when we learned something, heard something, or had something happen to us where we came face-to-face with the reality of the darkness of sin in the world, times when we longed for innocence because what we were encountering as we grew up seemed too difficult to face.

It seems strange to link the recognition of sin in the world to the cultivation of joy, but as we've seen, our God doesn't tend to follow patterns that commonly make sense. Paul says above that he is in "tears" recalling those who "live as enemies of the cross of Christ." He notes the characteristics of these people as destruction, self-indulgence, glorifying shameful things, and focusing on things of this world. Now, before we get all self-righteous, it is essential to remember that we were all this way at some point and that we serve a patient, gracious, and merciful God who does not want to lose any of His children. Just because someone fits those categories at some point, does not mean they always will.

Cultivating joy from the realization of sin in the world comes in three ways. One, Paul gives direct instruction to "keep your eyes on those who live as we do." Anyone who has watched the evening news knows the sadness that can come from hearing about unimaginable pain and suffering. But Paul tells us that we can't stay focused on what is wrong with the world all the time. While we are not called to stick our heads in the sand, we also can't spend hours devoted to ingesting the horrors created by evil and expect to have encouragement for our own lives. We have to keep our eyes on those who share our values, who "walk the walk," who bring us encouragement by the way they live. We cultivate joy by not immersing our minds in a constant study of the sin around us. Secondly, he reminds us that our citizenship is heaven. When the difficulties of this world seem too much to bear, it is sometimes because this is never how the world was originally designed to be. Sin is what got us here. We aren't meant to be here forever, and some of the pain we feel is because we are "Homesick." We cultivate joy by recognizing that it will not always be this way and this is not our "Home."

We are neither to ignore nor have our minds captivated by a fallen, sinful world. We are simply to recognize it.

The third one, which feels a little bit upside down, is that we should be aware of the sin in this world—and in ourselves—so as to not be surprised when we encounter it. Consider the command Jesus gave His disciples as He sent them out: *"I am sending you out like sheep among wolves. Therefore be as shrewd as snakes and as innocent as doves"* (Matthew 10:16). While I am not suggesting that we become jaded and untrusting of others, there is something to be said for grasping how lost people can get and letting those stories lose a bit of their shock value. "But, I don't want those things to lose shock value! I don't want pretend to 'accept' the difficult things of this world!" I get it. As a rose-colored-glasses-wearing, sparkles-celebrating, blushing-at-almost-anything gal, really, I get it. But let me see if I can sell you on something…

If you move to a place in your heart where you can recognize the sin in this world for what it is, you can better cope with your shock when your best friend comes to you and says she has had an affair. If you recognize the sin in this world, you can better manage your pain and be present for someone who has just lost their child in a drunk-driving accident. If you recognize the sin in this world, you can move faster toward love and forgiveness than if you have put people far too high up on a pedestal. If you recognize the sin in this world, you can be aware of how far, and how quickly, you too can fall and accept God's grace if you do.

Jesus never pretended that sin—dare I say rampant evil—did not exist. In fact, He talked about it regularly and used it as a way to guide people to Him. True joy is cultivated only in the realm of authenticity. We gain joy when we are engaged with authentic others who encourage us by the way they live for Christ. We gain joy when we realize the truth that our lives on Earth are merely a caricature of what is to be. And we gain the ability to better retain and offer joy when we recognize how fallen things are so that we can love and serve others from a place of truth. Our sinful fallen world is a reality. We better learn how to be here.

"Lord Jesus, this is a hard one to get my head wrapped around at times. Show me how to adopt your command to be 'as shrewd as snakes and as innocent as doves.' Let me live in joy that is authentic as I truly realize how fallen the world is. Help me to love others better as I see them through Your eyes and bring me people who are an encouragement when the difficulties around me feel like too much. Fill me with peace as You remind me that my work here is temporary, for I am not yet Home."

Reflection Questions:

On the spectrum from ignoring the sin of the world to letting it dominate my thoughts, where am I in recognizing the reality of our fallen world?

_____

_____

_____

_____

_____

What is something that brings me to tears and feels like "too much to bear"?

_____

_____

_____

_____

_____

How might I be better equipped to love people if I came to recognize the sin of the world as it is?

_____

_____

_____

_____

_____

How does Jesus' example of acknowledging sin encourage me to possibly change the way I think about fallen people or situations?

_____

_____

_____

_____

_____

Day 16, *Philippians 4:4-7 (Thankfulness in Difficulty)*

⁴ Rejoice in the Lord always. I will say it again: Rejoice! ⁵ Let your gentleness be evident to all. The Lord is near. ⁶ Do not be anxious about anything, but in every situation, by prayer and petition, with thanksgiving, present your requests to God. ⁷ And the peace of God, which transcends all understanding, will guard your hearts and your minds in Christ Jesus.

This is one of those days when God's commands to us feel like the spiritual equivalent of a lobotomy. However, no matter how challenging His words may be, we know that they are carefully and divinely chosen, so we can't go about wondering if that's *really* what He meant. Taking Jesus' menu a la carte throws the integrity of Scripture right out the window.

With that in mind, we'll dive in to some strong, all-encompassing statements about how to cultivate joy regardless of our situations. He begins with a pretty straightforward command: *"Rejoice in the Lord always."* Lobotomy #1. Always?!! Yes. Everyone, at some point, has to make the decision about whether or not God is good despite what is going on around them or in their lives. If we are not sure He is a God worth rejoicing over, that will color every command He gives us because we aren't quite sure if He can be trusted. If this is where you are with God, then start right here! Ask Him to grow you in this area, to show you why you may not trust Him, to guide you through the pain that may have led you to this place. Ask Him to lead you to the joy that comes from believing wholeheartedly that He is good even if other things are not. Figuring out how you feel about God's goodness is essential to being able to move forward with everything He asks us to do or believe.

The degree to which we believe in God's goodness is directly related to our ability to trust Him.

With that overarching concept in place, Paul then takes the opportunity to show us a spiritual recipe for dealing with anxiety. This process has always been fascinating to me and, thematically again, is seemingly backward from what is expected. There is an initial part of the solution for anxiety that seems to make sense. *"Do not be anxious about anything, but in every situation, by prayer and petition...present your requests to God."* In short, pray about it. This seems logical. Lift your burdens to the Lord. No matter what is going on, petition Him for strength, for help, for resolution to your challenges. Makes sense. However, He then throws in Lobotomy #2 by adding the phrase "with thanksgiving." Hold the phone. You want us offer thanksgiving for those things that breed anxiety? How are we supposed to do that?!

It makes sense to be frustrated in difficult situations if we believe that they are random, that God has abandoned us, or that a situation has no purpose and God is not in it. But thankfully, we do not serve a God who ignores us as He carelessly plays with time and eternity! All throughout Scripture He demonstrates His great love for us and His desire for intimate involvement in our lives. The thankfulness we offer in these anxiety-provoking situations comes out of our belief that He is with us as we experience them.

It's hard to thank someone for something if you think it was given to you, or allowed in your life, by someone who does not have your best interest in mind. As stated at the beginning, this is one of the deepest cruces of faith faced by anyone who decides to follow Jesus. Do you believe that He is good? Always? Regardless of the situation? And can that let you thank Him for anything, anytime, anywhere because you believe in His goodness? If we can really get to this point, then the joy comes along with the last verse when, *"…the peace of God, which transcends all understanding, will guard your hearts and your minds in Christ Jesus."* Turns out a spiritual lobotomy that allows us to trust Him and thank Him in any situation will allow peace in our lives that transcends all logical understanding. Many of the things that happen in this world do not make sense. We need His peace to transcend our logic.

"Lord, I fully admit that I cannot be free of anxiety unless You change my mind. Change my mind to trust You. Change my mind to believe in Your goodness. Change my mind so that I can say, 'No matter what.' This will never make sense in my earthly mind; there are too many terrible things to consider. Only You in Your infinite understanding can see how tragedy works together for good. I need Your peace and help to believe that is true."

Reflection Questions:

On a scale of 1-10 (10 being all the time), how able am I to rejoice in the Lord "always"?

_____

_____

_____

_____

_____

What are the things that keep me from being able to move closer to a 10?

_____

_____

_____

_____

_____

What are some things in my life that I am anxious about?

_____

_____

_____

_____

_____

Offer a prayer to the Lord here about something that makes you anxious, asking Him to increase your trust in Him and your ability to be thankful in the midst of these challenges.

_____

_____

_____

_____

_____

Week Five

Day 17, *Philippians 4:8-9 (Intentionality & Positive Mindset)*

[8] Finally, brothers and sisters, whatever is true, whatever is noble, whatever is right, whatever is pure, whatever is lovely, whatever is admirable—if anything is excellent or praiseworthy—think about such things. [9] Whatever you have learned or received or heard from me, or seen in me—put it into practice. And the God of peace will be with you.

Unlike the seemingly contrary task discussed in the last lesson, today's verses bring us something that feels a bit more commonsensical. Today Paul asks us to focus on things that are inherently enjoyable to increase our wellbeing. On a modern note, this practice of focusing on the positive is well supported through research by clinicians such as Dr. Martin Seligman. In the late 1990's, he made the unconventional move from studying the minority of people who were mentally ill, to instead examining the practices of those who were flourishing. This shift has produced research and practices that have drastically changed the way we approach medical, wellness, and mental health practices.

"What has been will be again, what has been done will be done again; there is nothing new under the sun" (Ecclesiastes 1:9). "New" ideas and conceptual frameworks for how to better live our lives come out all the time, but anything that truly works usually mirrors concepts in Scripture. This is not surprising as God designed us and of course knows what allows us to live our best for Him. Seeing Paul outline concepts from Dr. Seligman's research in Biblical text is a treat. I imagine God smiling as we move our science further into the understanding of His words as He says, "Told ya so."

So, what's the "told you so" for today that is supported by the positive psychology movement? In short, to focus on the good stuff! In order to cultivate joy through our mindset, Paul provides a straightforward list of things to be at the center of our thinking: 1) what is true, 2) what is noble, 3) what is right, 4) what is pure, 5) what is lovely, 6) what is admirable, 7) what is excellent, 8) what is praiseworthy. He is telling us to set our minds on what God says is accurate, to think about those things that are still beautiful and pure in our fallen world, to relish in the stories of those who are engaging in exceptional acts of love and service. While this straightforward command seems easily said, it is far less easily done.

If we want to cultivate joy by our mindset, we have to be intentional. Immediately following the list of positive focuses, Paul hands us the keys to making a positive mindset a habit. *"Whatever you have learned or received or heard from me, or seen in me – put it into practice. And the God of peace will be with you."* While positive psychology advocates for optimism, research also shows that optimism is learned. And if optimism is learned, so is pessimism, and helplessness, and every other pattern of thinking that drives our perceptions. Paul says we have to practice those things he has taught us and thinking positively is no exception.

Practice makes progress.

As explored in previous lessons, the culture we are in does not lend itself to focusing on those things that are positive. Intentionally changing our mindset to focus on the positive may require some significant changes to the patterns (or people!) in our lives so that we have the opportunity to "practice" being positive, and our practice can eventually become a habit. As a practical tip, I would encourage you to think about how you learn best (i.e., visually, auditorily, kinetically) to discern what may best help shift your mind in a positive direction. For a visual learner this may be a written reminder in the kitchen or on the bathroom mirror with a list of blessings or the choice to search the Internet for "happy news" for a positive read. For the auditory learner this may be a podcast that is uplifting or a conversation with an encouraging friend. For the kinetic processor this may be listing what you are grateful for during a run or creating a word board where you manipulate the magnets to create a new statement of gratitude each day. Make the changes that work for you.

Today's lesson reminds us to lean heavily on how God has designed us. We are creatures of habit and, positive or negative, habits are hard to break. Creating a habit of positivity requires practice, and our practices are going to be more effective if we do them according to how God has designed us to learn. We put these things into practice, not as a checklist, but as a recognition that the God of the universe who designed us also wrote our owner's manual. We are going to run most efficiently if we follow the Manufacturer's recommendations.

"Lord, it is easy to see how focusing on positive things may help me cultivate joy; however, that is far less easy to do with all of the negativity around me! Show me ways I can begin to focus on those things that fit Paul's list and the practices or people I may need to distance myself from, so I can get in some practice time. Thank You for designing me exactly as I am, and show me how to operate within this plan."

Reflection Questions:

Create a list of things, situations, or relationships that match up with Paul's list of positives: 1) what is true, 2) what is noble, 3) what is right, 4) what is pure, 5) what is lovely, 6) what is admirable, 7) what is excellent, 8) what is praiseworthy.

_____

_____

_____

_____

_____

What are some things I already do that contribute to having a positive mindset?

_____

_____

_____

_____

_____

What are the biggest obstacles I face when attempting to have a positive mindset?

_____

_____

_____

_____

_____

When considering how I learn best, what is something I can begin today that would help to focus my mind in a positive direction and give me the opportunity to turn a practice into a habit?

_____

_____

_____

_____

_____

Day 18, *Philippians 4:10-13 (Contentment)*

¹⁰ I rejoiced greatly in the Lord that at last you renewed your concern for me. Indeed, you were concerned, but you had no opportunity to show it. ¹¹ I am not saying this because I am in need, for I have learned to be content whatever the circumstances. ¹² I know what it is to be in need, and I know what it is to have plenty. I have learned the secret of being content in any and every situation, whether well fed or hungry, whether living in plenty or in want. ¹³ I can do all this through him who gives me strength.

As a coach's wife, sports fan, and athlete I think I may have known Philippians 4:13 long before I had any idea what a relationship with Jesus was. It is the verse that people write on their arms and legs during marathons, on vision boards during labor, and in journals during hours of chemotherapy. There are simply some verses that stand alone and bring strength to God's people in just a handful of words.

Today, however, we are going to take a glance at surrounding words that accompany this popular verse. Paul spends the words leading up to verse 13 discussing contentment. He says that he has learned to be content "whatever the circumstances" and "in any and every situation." While those phrases alone would have been enough to cover everything, he goes further by offering an extra little bit of wisdom with specific examples. Paul says that he has learned to be content when in need *and* when he has plenty, when hungry *and* well fed. How wise of him to note that contentment is a necessary component even when everything is going well. I am so grateful he offers this caveat because it lets us explore the possibility that even in those times when we are full with everything we could need, we may still lack contentment if we don't find our fulfillment in Christ.

While experiencing a lack of contentment when "hungry" or "in need" seems to make sense, being discontent when we are "well fed" and have "plenty" initially seems counterintuitive. No matter how upside down this may seem at first, it does not take much to think of people who have all they could ever need, yet they are miserable. To bring it even closer to home, I am betting we can all think of times when we were more than provided for, yet we experienced feelings of discontentment.

As we have explored in previous lessons, feelings of discontentment tend to stem from feeling as though we don't have "enough." Advertisements suggest that we don't have enough stuff or that it isn't the right kind. Spending a great deal of time on social media can create discontentment as we look at the hand-picked photos and polished lives of others who have the relationship, the children, the education, the trips and vacations, the crafts and the cooking, the talents or opportunities that we think we need. For some, being content with plenty may be a harder task than being content with little. Sometimes when we are in need and stripped of our reliance on other things, we can see with greater clarity that God is all we have to rely on. When living in the land of wealth and opportunity, it is easier to be seduced by the illusion that contentment is coming or may come from something other than God.

Contentment is a gift easily broken by our wants.

Regardless of whether we are living in plenty or in need, the answer to cultivating joy and contentment is the same. Check out the sentence preceding verse 13, *"I have learned the secret of being content in any and every situation, whether well fed or hungry, whether living in plenty or in want."* The secret? *"I can do all things through him who gives me strength."* Amazing. This verse that we have been using all these years only to ask for strength in challenging situations is actually tied to contentment. I can be content when I have desperate need, and I can be content when I have blessings coming out of my ears because *He* gives me the strength to do so. The same God who gives us the strength to fight, persevere, and struggle through hardship is the same one who gives us the strength to be content no matter our situation.

I want you to consider today if there are situations in your life where you may have been attempting to utilize God's strength in an active, uphill, struggling way…the way we may have traditionally used Philippians 4:13. Consider if there may be space in that situation to use that verse not only for strength but also to bring about contentment. God's strength is given to us just as much to fight as it is to cultivate joy by finding contentment in life as it currently is. Prayer that is "doubling down" on both aspects of 4:13 may sound like this:

"Lord, help me to rely on You in our struggles to pay our bills each month. I need Your strength to get up and get to work each day, but I need Your contentment to know that You will provide for us."

"Lord, help me to trust You as I raise my children. I need Your strength to face the daily struggle of disciplining them, encouraging them, and taking care of their needs, but I also need Your contentment to fill me knowing that You will take all of my efforts and multiply them as You love them and care for them."

See what it may do today if you accompany your pleas for strength from the Lord with prayer for strength to be content no matter your circumstances!

"Lord, You give us such a wonderful example in Paul who over the course of his life had known the highest of highs and the lowest of lows. It seems he had seen so many varied circumstances that he finally learned that You are the only consistent thing. Through Your strength alone could he be content no matter what his life was like at the time. While we continue to strive to live for You, give us joy through contentment in our current circumstances. Help us to know the strength of being able to say, 'It's okay.'"

Reflection Questions:

Reflect upon a time when you remember experiencing true contentment. What contributed to that feeling?

_____

_____

_____

_____

_____

What are some areas of my life where I struggle with contentment?

_____

_____

_____

_____

_____

As I review these things, does it appear as though I am struggling for contentment in plenty or in need?

_____

_____

_____

_____

_____

What aspect of my prayer life may be blessed by including a plea for contentment along with a plea for strength?

_____

_____

_____

_____

_____

Day 19, *Philippians 4:14-19 (Provision for Others)*

¹⁴ Yet it was good of you to share in my troubles. ¹⁵ Moreover, as you Philippians know, in the early days of your acquaintance with the gospel, when I set out from Macedonia, not one church shared with me in the matter of giving and receiving, except you only; ¹⁶ for even when I was in Thessalonica, you sent me aid more than once when I was in need. ¹⁷ Not that I desire your gifts; what I desire is that more be credited to your account. ¹⁸ I have received full payment and have more than enough. I am amply supplied, now that I have received from Epaphroditus the gifts you sent. They are a fragrant offering, an acceptable sacrifice, pleasing to God. ¹⁹ And my God will meet all your needs according to the riches of his glory in Christ Jesus.

²⁰ To our God and Father be glory for ever and ever. Amen.

²¹ Greet all God's people in Christ Jesus. The brothers and sisters who are with me send greetings. ²² All God's people here send you greetings, especially those who belong to Caesar's household.

²³ The grace of the Lord Jesus Christ be with your spirit. Amen.

Our final look at the book of Philippians will charge us with a call to cultivate joy for ourselves and others through provision. Paul spends time in the first part of today's Scripture simply thanking the Philippian people for being there for him as he has continued in his ministry elsewhere. He shares here that in those early days the people at Philippi were the only ones who were supporting him. It appears as though they likely offered encouragement to him emotionally as well as physically and financially. It is easy to imagine that Paul may have felt very lonely in his efforts if only one of the churches he had invested in was continuing to communicate with him or support the work he was doing. He wanted to take the time to let the church at Philippi know how much it meant to him that they remembered him and provided for him.

No matter how many friends and family we have, it is a great joy to feel as though people are intentionally supporting us. Moreover, we have a call on our lives to support and meet the needs of others. It is one thing to engage in a casual relationship; it is quite another to do as the Philippians did for Paul and "share in his troubles." Sharing in someone's troubles means that you are a) paying enough attention to know when they are in trouble and b) intentionally using what you have been given in Christ to bless them. As Paul's example suggests, even if it seems as though people are well connected, it may be that you are someone's "only" as the Philippian church was for Paul. We need to increase our awareness of other's needs and consider what it is that we may have to offer others to provide for them out of all that God has given us.

As we talked about on day 17, each of us is uniquely designed by God. We each have different talents, treasures, and gifts that we can use to provide for others. To illustrate, I will provide what is an amusing, albeit self-deprecating, personal example. I can't cook. Truly, I've tried. Every time someone goes through a tragedy or has a baby and we are asked to sign up to bring the family meals, I either try to blend into the wall or sign up with the full intention of bringing something from a restaurant. No one will be blessed by me trying to stock their freezer with my attempt at lasagna. However, you know what I do have? Professional training as a counselor. Thursdays off. A love of walking outdoors. A house with an extra bedroom. That means I can listen and encourage. I can use my day off to take care of an errand, a need, or someone's cable service call. I can take a friend for a walk, so we can be side by side as she talks about something that is too hard for a face-to-face conversation. I can invite someone to spend the night in a safe and comfortable home.

All that we have been given is an overflow of God's love.

As we close out our study of Paul's letter to the Philippians, let's take the opportunity to figure out how we are going to pay forward what we have learned. Consider how God has uniquely designed you and your circumstances to provide for the needs of others. Cultivate joy by investing in the needs of others and seeing how God blesses those efforts. Pray for people who may see and meet your needs while also seeking to help those around you. If Paul needed people, then certainly we all do. Let's seek to be those provisional people today.

"Lord, You have provided for me in so many ways. Help me to take an inventory of this, so I may praise You and also seek to extend the fruits of those blessings to others. I thank You for the unique ways I can provide for others, and I also thank You for the needs I have so as to allow others to use their gifts of provision as well. You are a generous and sacrificial God. Help me to follow Your example in my own life."

Reflection Questions:

Reflect on what it may have been like for Paul to be pouring himself out in service to others and receiving very little support back.

_____

_____

_____

_____

_____

What talents, treasures, or gifts do I have that I could use to bless others?

_____

_____

_____

_____

_____

Name one person or opportunity where I can use what I have to provide for someone this week.

_____

_____

_____

_____

_____

Offer God a need you have and pray that He would provide for a way to have that need filled.

_____

_____

_____

_____

_____

Day 20, *Reflection*

Well, friends, we have been through a quick but hopefully powerful journey together! Today's lesson will be shorter but hopefully allow you an opportunity to think more comprehensively about all that we have learned. Thank you for your perseverance and commitment to seeing this through to the end. I am hopeful that the perspectives Paul shared with us are ones you can implement in your daily life to better cultivate joy.

As we have wandered through the book of Philippians there have been some recurring themes including finding your identity and value solely in Christ, being reminded that we "aren't that big of a deal," utilizing God's strength rather than our own to serve people, and understanding the power of learning and friendships. I bet there are others you may have been touched by that I didn't even think of! What themes or points of understanding were most influential for you during this study?

_____

_____

_____

_____

_____

Now that we are at the end of what Paul wanted to share with us, I am wondering what it is that you are most excited to pay forward to other people. Consider whether you have been inspired by an idea to begin work on a project, by a concept that will help you better care for a friend, or by a practice that will yield dividends not only for yourself but also for the lives of those around you. In short, what information or Scripture did you study that affected change in you?

_____

_____

_____

_____

_____

And finally, we take the opportunity to claim the promises of God that we have learned these past five weeks and make some commitments of our own. What are the most important points you want to hang on to from this study as you move forward in your life with Christ? Offer a prayer below claiming His promise to "finish a good work in you" and ask for His help remembering and committing to the information you have learned and the changes you want to make.

_____

_____

_____

_____

_____

"Sweet Jesus, I thank You for those who have journeyed here together. I pray that they are blessed beyond measure by the words You inspired Paul to share. Give them strength as they live for You and let them know how deeply and perfectly You love them. Show them how to cultivate joy directly from You and fill their moments with a peaceful awareness of Your Spirit. Thank you for loving each of us. We are grateful."